Finding Hope in Changing Seasons

a collection of poetry

Victoria Grace Gehman

Who Is This Book For?

This book is for those who've found hope in the midst of difficult, changing seasons.

And this book is also for those who long for – but are afraid to – look for hope in a current chaotic season.

I hope this book speaks to your soul, letting you know you are not alone.

And I hope you will allow me to hold on to hope for you until you're able to hold on to your own hope.

Copyright Information

Finding Hope in Changing Seasons: a collection of poems
This is a collection of poems, based on my own or a loved one's experiences and
thoughts and feelings about those experiences.

Book Cover Design by Madeline Gehman

Note About Photos: All photographs throughout the book were taken by me personally. None of the images used were pulled from the internet, and no one else owns rights to any of the photos used.

Book Description

If you've struggled with chronic pain, mental health challenges, and/or burnout, you may relate to the poems shared in this book. Using poetry, this book exploresways I've learned to care for myself and cling to hope as I navigated new and
changing seasons of life.

Following a medical leave and health issues which eventually led me to take a break from my career in social work and return to food service at a local café, I found myself confused and struggling with various emotions. However, through this difficult season, I began to rediscover things that brought me joy and helped me to appreciate being alive: Writing. Rescuing a dog. Spending time outdoors. Consistent fresh air and exercise. Intentionality in frienships. Quiet moments of stillness.
In this book I share reflections on my struggles, ways I learned to care for myself, and how I found hope even in this new season. I hope it encourages youin whatever season you may find yourself.

I also share nature photography on each page of this book. This is my unique trademark, so to speak, that I also used in my first book. Using nature photos as background is a way to not only brighten up the pages, but it also allows me to
combine my passions for writing and nature photography.

Reflections in the Struggles

Victoria Grace Gehman

Ever Be the Same

And I don't think,
I will ever be the same after this
And honestly,
I am okay with this.
In fact, I hope
That I will never go back.
Back to the shadows where I used to live,
When things were regularly dark.
So dark that I could not see
Even my hand in front of me.

Victoria Grace Gehman

These Walls

Brick by brick,
Layer upon layer,
I build these walls.
I can't let you in.
I build and build until there is no way in.
And then for good measure–
I add barbed wire along the top.
And as if that weren't good enough–
I secure padlocks on the sturdy, metal doors.
No one is getting in.
No one but me
Even has a spare key.
I won't let you in.
I can't.
It took me years to build these walls
and secure them just so–
I can't destroy them now.
For I can't do this again.
I used to let people in...
But that was before they ruined my walls.
They left deep bruises and ugly scars.
So many times that not a single brick
was left untouched, unharmed.

I tried and I'm done trying.

For there are only so many times one can repair a wall.

Before it crumbles,

Leaving you exposed and vulnerable to the elements–

To predators.

To those who would shatter your trust yet again.

3

Victoria Grace Gehman

<u>Where Do I Fit?</u>

And as I sit,
I wonder where I fit.
Because I know for sure I don't fit here—
Maybe I don't fit anywhere, I fear.
These brightly polished, perfectly put-together spaces.
All these happy, smiling faces.
They leave no room for authenticity.
There is no real vulnerability.
They make it feel like perfection is a requirement.
So I just stay silent.
Because I don't feel anywhere close to perfect; I feel bro-
ken.
So much hurt is left unspoken.
How many of us don't ever return?
Because we yearn
For something more real,
To not have to hide how we feel.
We long for safe spaces,
For a community that embraces
All of us—
Regardless of our gender or our race,
Regardless of our past or our mistakes,
Regardless of our political affiliation or our beliefs,

Regardless of our health or our griefs–
We are all human,
Every single one of us.
Where does this exist?
Where do we fit?

Victoria Grace Gehman

Nighttime

Day turns to night–
Slowly, but surely.
Just as surely as the sun rises,
It sets.
Darkness settles.
This is when my thoughts begin to swirl around my brain–
Dark and unsettling.
Chaotic and threatening.
I can't sleep.
I can't breathe.
There is no relief.
I long for the light.
And yet,
When the tossing and turning is finally over,
When my restless dozing has led to morning once again–
I dread the new day.
I despise the sun–
The light I longed for just hours ago–
Because it now reminds me that I am still alive for another
day.
And I did not want to be alive for another day.
I wanted to drift into oblivion.

To never awake.
Light, dark–
It all feels harsh.
Life, death–
I hate that I can't breathe and yet, I want this to be my
last breath.

<u>You Don't Have a Clue</u>

And you don't have a clue
The pain I've been through.
And you don't have a clue
That I have scars, too.
And you don't have a clue
What I wouldn't do for you.
And you don't have a clue
How much I wish this mess I could undo.
And you don't have a clue
The real reason why I withdrew.
And you don't have a clue
How much it hurts when you say things that are untrue.
And you don't have clue
How much I want a redo.
You don't have a clue.

Fight for Me

I wanted you to fight for me.
I didn't think you'd give up so easily.
Just once, I wanted to be pursued.
Instead of feeling used and abused.
I feel betrayed yet again.
Will anyone ever fight for me, and when?
All the times I thought you cared,
All the memories we've shared—
Did it all mean nothing to you?
How did I not have a clue?
I guess you're just like all the rest.
Giving up on me is what you do best.
I wanted you to fight for me.
I really thought you'd be the one to see...

I Wonder

And I wonder.
I wonder if you grow weary of my struggling.
I wonder.
If you wonder
If I'll ever be okay.
I wonder if someday you'll loosen your grip on me,
Until slowly, you no longer see me at all.
Or care whether I ever will be okay.
And I wonder
Why I have to wonder so much.

<u>Sometimes I Wonder</u>

Sometimes I wonder,
Do you still think about me?
Do you wish you would have done something differently?
That you could go back and apologize?
Or was my leaving just good riddance to you?
I want to try again,
But I don't know if I can.
To take that risk ... It feels too risky.
Because if I trust and get wounded so deeply another time,
I just might break– to the point of no return.

Rock Bottom

Sometimes we have to reach rock bottom
In order to take that first step towards healing.
If things never got this dark and out of control,
Would we have made those drastic, hard decisions–
The ones that felt so life-altering and crushing,
But ended up being so healing and good.
The decisions that ended up saving us.
After the initial grief and gut-wrenching sobs,
As life as we knew it collapsed before our eyes.
After wondering if we were just a failure.
After determining we didn't want to live any longer.
After falling into a deep, dark pit,
With no way out.
We couldn't see the light.
We thought that this was the end of life.
Until slowly, as we learned to allow our body
and our soul to rest,
As we slept long hours,
And became vulnerable about our struggles,
As we honestly sought help,
And learned to sit with the emotions,
Instead of shying away from them,
As we began to rediscover our passions and hobbies,

Instead of overworking and burying our pain,
Slowly, slowly,
We began to find peace and to rediscover hope,
And a joy in living.
We learned to appreciate stillness,
And eventually, we realized
We had made progress—
We were finally healing—
From the trauma and the burnout.
We will never be whole, but we can be healthier.
The light has appeared;
We just needed to slow down and allow someone to take us
by the hand and lead us back,
Back to where the light pours in.

Victoria Grace Gehman

<u>Maybe Both Could Be True</u>

As I reach this intersection,
I turn right instead of left.
And it just feels right.
Yet, there is still an ache in my heart.
Still doubts, and fears, and unanswered questions,
And that lingering whisper saying, "You failed. You we-
ren't good enough."
I don't regret my time in child welfare,
But I also don't regret resigning to go work at a café.
Maybe it is possible that both those things could be true—
At the same time.
Maybe this is right for me right now, in this season.
But maybe it's okay that I still struggle with not getting
the social work jobs I applied for.
Still struggle with needing to leave a job that I wanted to
remain in.
Maybe the joy in this new season
Can coexist with the grief over all that my health issues
have caused me to lose.

<u>Panic Attack</u>

Gasping for air,
Stabbing chest pains,
Feeling like I'm dying,
Thinking surely this must be a heart attack,
Anxiety is controlling,
And I don't have a freaking clue what's even wrong–
This is what a panic attack feels like for me.
And every time I think I get a breather,
It's like I am pulled back under,
Gasping for air all over again–
Until my lungs hurt
And pangs stab my chest.
I'm on the brink of exhaustion.
I can't sleep.
I. Just. Want. Air.

Victoria Grace Gehman

When I'm Not There

When I'm not there,
Please don't try to guilt me under the guise of care.
Instead, ask if I am okay,
Because what usually keeps me away
Is what people say,
Or how they don't stay
When I reveal the broken parts
That I kept buried inside my heart.
I long for community,
But some days I just don't have the capacity
To deal with the judgment, the questions, the hurtful
words.
I just need to be heard.
To be seen and loved as I am,
For I am doing the best I can.
Please don't tell me I have to be more happy to be here.
I want to be welcomed even in my fear,
In my doubts, and in my pain,
I want to know my efforts are not in vain.
I want to believe that there is room for me here,
And yet, people continue to confirm my fear
That I am not welcomed here—
Or there.

Or maybe anywhere.

Or at least that is what the doubts creeping in try to tell
me.

And yet there must be someone who hears my plea?

Let there be room for the broken,

Let there be rest for the weary,

Let there be weights lifted from the heavy-hearted.

Let there be presence in the waiting,

Empathy in the pain,

Grace in the failures,

Hope to carry on.

To show up next time

Feeling a little less broken and a little more hope

Because we are not shamed or judged or ignored–

But welcomed.

Even if we don't fit the norm.

Victoria Grace Gehman

Unknowns

How many questions go unanswered.
How long we must wait.
So much remains unknown in this big, scary world.
We want to know.
We scream and shout, making our need to know be known.
But we are met with only quiet stillness.
No answers come. Only silence.
But what if there is knowing in the stillness?
What if the things we most need to know come through
quiet?
In the stillness,
Through the countless stars in the sky,
And the gentle rustling of leaves,
There is a small whisper,
Reminding us that we are fully known.
And we serve a God who knows all of our unknowns.
He won't be surprised,
And though we wish that he would tell us what comes
next,
There is comfort in the stillness to remember that
He knows–
He knows us. He knows our needs, our fears, our doubts.
And He knows what comes next.

Sit in the stillness and learn to be okay not knowing.
Because if there were no unknowns, there would be less
beauty.
Because sometimes the scariest unknowns
Turn out to be the most beautiful.

A Few Steps Forward, and a Step Back

Four steps forward, then two steps back;
Five steps forward, then one step back–
The backwards steps are fewer than the forward ones, so
why are they
the ones I'm focusing on?
Backwards, and forward.
Forward, and backwards.
It's all part of life.
We think our one step back is somehow powerful enough to
cancel out all the many forward steps we've taken.
But why are we giving one misstep so much power?
And why do we give such little value to all those forward
steps?
Why are we so quick to diminish them?
When it took us so much effort and courage to get there in
the first place.
Each step forward counts–
No matter how tiny.
And the occasional backwards tumbles do not erase all that
progress.
If you're climbing a mountain and you lose your footing
and fall a few steps–
Do you have to start all over?
No, you just have to climb back up those few steps.
You didn't lose all the progress–
You just have to climb back up a few steps
And then keep on going. So give yourself some grace.

Too Good to Be True

It just feels so good–
And things, for me, are rarely good.
So it seems too good to be true.
Do I dare to believe there could be happiness for me?
A future where I'm not alone?
With a person who doesn't think I am too much?
Like I said, seems too good to be true.
But what if some good things do come true?
What if not all truth hurts?
Leave room for those what ifs or you'll miss the good–
And then you may never find out if it could have been true–
Both true and good.

Victoria Grace Gehman

When a Writer Can't Find the Words

Some days, when I sit down to write,
the words flow freely—
Faster than I can possibly get them onto paper or typed on
the computer,
Even though I am a pretty fast typer.
Other days,
I sit down,
And nothing.
I have so much floating around in my mind,
But the words won't form.
I'm a writer, and yet I can't seem to write anything.
Some days, the heaviness and the hard makes it so much
easier to write,
And other days it steals my motivation.
Sometimes, when I'm happy,
I don't know what to say.
Because, to be honest, I'm better at being sad.
Maybe you can relate.
But then other days,
I find a burst of joy so strong that I feel I must share it
with the world.
I guess what I'm saying is—
There are days when even our biggest passions feel far off.
If you're having an off day, or even an off week or month,
It doesn't make you a failure.
It just makes you human.

Let Me Free

Pressed against the window,
Trees fly by
And I wonder why–
Why won't you let me go.
I long to just disappear, be free.
Allowing the vast forest to swallow me,
The bubbling brook bringing me security,
Making me feel at peace,
Washing away my worries,
Cleansing my scars as they sting with the cold water,
As it splashes against me,
A welcome distraction.
Here, by the brook, I can unhook
All these burdens that I carry,
Here, I let them loose,
And feel the cool air and the warm sunshine,
Welcoming me to safety and rest.
And freedom.

Faith, Flannels, and the Forest

Trudging through this muddy path in the woods,
Coffee cup in hand,
Flannel shirt providing warming comfort—
Here, I begin to find myself again.
To remember that I have not walked these paths alone.
My faith has carried me.
Even when I tried to run from it,
It pulled me back.
In the same way that I am pulled back to the woods time
and time again
With this unexplainable, unignorable tug—
I am pulled back to my faith,
My roots.
These tree roots remind me of my own roots.
The ones I worked to cultivate in easier times—
So that in these dark moments which are sure to continue
repeating themselves,
I would not be left with nothing to cling to—
No roots to keep me attached.
Even when I stumble, forgetting these roots are here,
There is Someone watching over me.
And He sees me through the opening in the trees above,
He sees me when the sun is shining,

And He sees me when the rain is pouring.
And He remains. Even through the storms.
So I will keep trudging,
Though this flannel may rip on the branches, and the forest
may get dark,
I will not stop.
Until I return to my roots yet again.

Victoria Grace Gehman

Death

Unwelcome. Unexpected.
And not the fun kind of unexpected– like a promotion or a
timely gift or a visit from a friend we'd missed–
But the awful kind.
It leaves you whirling around,
In shock. In disbelief.
Anger. Denial. Guilt.
Especially the guilt.
The guilt comes on like one of those unexpected storms–
When the sky was clear just a moment before.
Suddenly, you find yourself second-guessing everything,
Analyzing your last encounter with the person.
Should you have said something different?
What would you have done differently if you knew this
would be your last memory together?
And then there are all the questions:
Why?
Why them? Why now? Why in that way?
Just Why???
I think that is the main question we ask.
Because death just feels so unnatural.
And we cannot comprehend it.
We try to make sense of it,

But we just can't.
Because the loss leaves a gaping hole.
Grief–
It changes us.
And we will never be the same.
Maybe we turn to alcohol to cope.
Maybe we overwork to avoid the feelings and the sorrow.
Or maybe it changes us for the better–
And we vow to become a better person–
To love and cherish others more fully
while we have them with us.
Because we never know what day might be our last.
Maybe we are numb and feel nothing at all.
Or maybe the anger never leaves.
People try to put time limits on our grief,
But grief doesn't have a time limit.
It doesn't even run on regular time–
It runs on its own time.
And that clock ticks differently for everyone.

Victoria Grace Gehman

Splash Cold Water

I splash cold water on my face
Just in case
Maybe this isn't real.
But ugh– I can feel.
So I guess it must be real.
I thought I was finally going to heal.
I hoped it was a bad dream,
But now I want to scream.
This pain,
It's back again.
Even stronger than before,
It's a never-ending war.
So what the heck was the point of all this?
If I was going to sink right back into the abyss.

<u>Not Magically Healed</u>

After a surgery, for the first two weeks or so,
suddenly people care about you.
But after those two weeks, just as suddenly,
they go back to not caring.
As if you're magically healed.
But what if you're not?
And do they not understand recovery is not a
one-size-fits-all?
Nor does recovery suddenly end at two weeks.
The pain – over time, it may wane.
But those scars? They'll remain.
And we'll remember the ones who cared–
Beyond that two-week mark.

Victoria Grace Gehman

Diving Deep

Diving deep,
Into the trauma and the hurt,
It makes me weep
Under the water now— I'm immersed.
Thinking on what could have been
Feeling like I'm drowning
All these things I've seen—
Maybe I shouldn't have dove in.
And yet, without the deep dive,
I might never have reached this point of healing.
Slowly, I resurface— I'm coming alive.
Maybe someday the diving will have me thriving.
It's painful now, as I gasp for air.
But someday my story I'll be able to share.

Poisonous Words

You say you're comforting, but your words– they taste like
poison on my lips.
You say you care, but your words– they are daggers,
piercing my soul.
You say you're just trying to help, but your words,
your so-called help, it feels so harsh.
You say you understand, but if you really understood,
you'd just sit quietly with me.
Instead of blabbering on and on.
You say you didn't mean any harm, but then why did it feel
like you didn't mean any good either?
Your words, they are poison, acid burning inside me–
How do your words not burn your own throat as you utter
them?
May we learn to turn our words into a healing potion,
rather than poison.

Learning to Care for Myself

Victoria Grace Gehman

To My Body

It seems there's always something,
Always some new way for you to discourage me, wear me
down, and cause me pain.
Why do you hate me so?
When you hurt too much for me to complete basic tasks,
You leave me frustrated, depressed, exhausted.
When I can't go out with others my age because the price
I'll pay the next day is just too high,
It makes for such loneliness.
Why do you hate me so?
And yet.
I'm learning.
Slowly learning.
To honor your needs.
To allow you to rest.
To keep my eyes open for the cues you give me.
To listen for what you need.
You may not be like others,
But you're the only body I've got.
And I will do my best to care for you.

<u>Sorrows Fall Away</u>

My sorrows fall away, like leaves falling from their trees.
As soon as I smell that autumn air,
Survey the brilliance of the leaves.
I wonder – do the leaves worry about what comes next–
If they'll soon turn brown and be trampled underfoot,
destroyed.
Or if, perhaps, some child will collect and save them,
Turning them into something beautiful,
Something that will last through many more seasons.
Do I fret about what is next?
Or do I savor these moments of beauty, joy, and healing
As I change with the seasons,
As the old makes way for new,
As my body and soul experience healing,
Through and through.

Unreplaceable

There's a saying that goes something like,
"You're replaceable at work,
but you're not replaceable at home."
But what if you're the only one in your home?
What if you don't have a husband or kids or even a pet that
rely on you?
Are you really still unreplaceable?
When it's just me, myself, and I
It's easy to work late–
No one cares if you get home well after dark–
Even in the summertime,
when it doesn't get dark until very late.
No one is missing you.
No one is waiting on you to feed them.
So it seems that it doesn't really matter.
Or at least that is what you tell yourself,
To try to justify all the late nights.
But there is only one you.
And if your job is taking you away from you,
Compromising your health–
Physical or emotional–
Making you forget to eat,
Depleting you of joy,
Ensuring that you have no time
for healthy human connections,
Then yes, you're unreplaceable at home.
Even if it's "just" you.

Because you matter.
Ensuring that you have no time
for healthy human connections,
Then yes, you're unreplaceable at home.
Even if it's "just" you.
Because you matter.

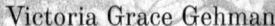

Victoria Grace Gehman

<u>Perfect Night</u>

Sound of the crackling campfire,
Crickets chirping,
Feel of the cool breeze and strong arms around me,
Comforting smell of the mountain air,
Delicious taste of roasted s'mores,
Marshmallow roasted to perfection,
Beauty of a thousand stars,
Watching over me,
I look up and smile.

My Own Company

Learning to be content in one's own company—
No longer always needing someone to accompany
I used to numb the emotions by always being busy,
rarely alone.
And yet still feeling so unknown.
To be alone meant to feel—
To allow oneself to begin to heal.
This felt scary,
But it all became too much to carry.
And through learning to embrace all the feeling,
I began healing.
Until being alone didn't feel so unbearable,
For now, I was finding I'm capable.
Able to enjoy my quiet, alone moments
Instead of seeing them as opponents.

Victoria Grace Gehman

The World Moves On

And it feels like the whole entire world
continues to move on–
While I'm still here: unsure, confused, uncertain.
Agencies, friends – they all move forward.
And Im still stuck.
Or maybe I am moving forward– but in a different way?
There's this guilt – as they carry on with MSWs, careers,
and degrees.
And I'm just, here. Cooking food. Taking inventory. Mana-
ging a kitchen.
But, mixed with the guilt, is a sense of peace, of happiness.
My life is slower now. I'm healing, my progress has truly
been astounding.
So, maybe I am right where I am meant to be.
In the quiet, in nature, there is peace.
Maybe I am meant to help others see that. If they would
only slow down, too...
And not worry so much about what we miss out on as the
world carries on?
What if, instead, the question is: what peace are we mis-
sing as we let the world drag us with it?
Maybe it's not me who's missing out.
Maybe it's them.
So, carry on, world.
I'll catch up when I am ready.

My Happy Place

It stretches for miles–
Both the forest and my imagination.
It is here where I can imagine the most
magical storylines–
Because here, in the forest–
Bubbling brooks, canopies of green,
bright swirling leaves–
Is the most magical of places.
I let loose my imagination,
As I let loose my dog to scamper and explore.
It's quiet and peaceful here.
Here, in solitude, I surrender–
To relax, let my creative juices flow.
I'm at peace within, and I feel peace all around me.
For here, in the forest, I can imagine that all is well
And I will never have to leave this magical space.

Victoria Grace Gehman

Things We Take for Granted

Things we so often take for granted,
Suddenly become treasures
After a life-changing situation.
A death, an operation, an accident, a loss of some kind.
An event that leaves you reeling.
Taking the things you've known and loved.
A week ago, I was walking for hours a day.
Now, today, I can barely walk five minutes
Before I need to stop.

Humbling and hurting.
Those are the words that most define these days.
And yet, in the pain and the humility,
I am finding new joy.
Treasuring the small things:
An ice cream cone,
A sunset drive,
The feel of the sunshine on my face,
The energy to read a few chapters of a book,
The ability to take just a four-minute walk.
Simple things.
Often-taken-for-granted things.
The wonder as I slowly lick my waffle cone and gaze up at
colorful leaves,
Resembles the wonder of a young child,
Experiencing those things for the very first time.

And I wonder:
When did we lose that wonder?

Victoria Grace Gehman

Be Gentle with Your Body

And if, today, you find your mind revolting against what
your body needs...
If you're tired of feeling useless,
And your mind keeps telling you it's all pointless.
If you're feeling stuck –
Trapped inside a body that's wracked by pain,
Trapped inside a mind that doesn't seem to quiet,
Trapped inside a building when all you want is to smell the
woods, to feel the crunch of leaves beneath your feet,
To wonder at the beauty of the color-changing leaves.
If you're growing weary of endless diagnoses, doctor appo-
intments,
depression, and disappointments,
If your questions sound like an elementary recitation of
pronouns–
Who, what, where, when, why?
Who can help? What is going on? Where can I find peace?
When will this end? Why do I have to endure this? –
If, today, these questions and feelings are yours,
You are not alone.
Your body feels like the enemy, I know.
But your body – she's courageous and resilient.
She's been through a lot,
And so have you.
She needs her rest,

And so do you.
I know it's inconvenient,
I know it makes you feel weak–
But this body–
She has wisdom and she knows you've got to stop–
Stop pushing through, trying to make it on your own.
Slow down and rest.
Let someone refill that coffee cup for you, wash your dishes, and walk your pup.
For you are worth this kind of care.

Victoria Grace Gehman

Memories and Job Changes

Because, as a caseworker, I drove all over the county,
There is hardly a road in this county that does not hold
some type of work memory.
As I drive around, whether for pleasure or purpose,
I still carry with me the heaviness of so much brokenness,
There are entire caseloads of people whom I'll never for-
get.
People I still hold compassion and empathy for.
People who I still think about regularly–
Wondering how they are doing, praying for them.
As I drive, I remember the emotions.
I remember the tightness of my chest and the anxiety as I
traveled to a difficult visit or court hearing.
I remember the tears,
as I drove home after a long, hard day–
Feeling like I couldn't do enough,
Worrying about the safety of kids.
It's a job that sticks with you.
Forever.
It changes you.
And while I may not be practicing social work
directly right now,
I still remember.
And I will never forget.
Being a social worker is a large part of who I am,
And those skills serve me well in any job.

I don't miss the stress,
And the longer I've been gone,
The more I see how unhealthy my life had become.
But I do miss the job.
And I do still care.
And I don't regret my time there.
But stepping away has opened up space for me to pursue
my passions in other ways.
It has allowed me to have the capacity to use my empathy
and skills in new ways—
Life-giving ways—
Ways that I wasn't able to utilize those skills before, when
my job consumed my whole life
And there was no space left to even contemplate much else.
Through writing, speaking, advocating, inspiring,
and being a safe presence for people who are hurting.

Victoria Grace Gehman

Some Days

Some days, we feel competent.
Some days, we believe we are a failure.
Some days, the smile we put on is real.
Some days, we're not actually as "put together" as we look.
Some days, we enjoy life.
Some days, we don't feel we can carry on
for another moment, let alone another day.
Some days, we dress up and go out.
Some days, we put on oversized sweatshirts and curl up in
a ball, not moving from the bed or the couch
For hours at a time.
Some days, we care for ourselves and expect care from
others.
Some days, we don't feel as though we deserve love and
care.
Some days, we accomplish much.
Some days, we lay in bed.
Some days, we see the light.
Some days, only darkness is near, the light hidden by gray
clouds refusing to make space for the sun.
Some days, we feel happy.
Some days, we grieve and feel anger or sadness.
Some days, we are physically able to do more.
Some days, our bodies demand we take the day off, even
when that isn't a realistic option.
Some days, we are content and at peace.

Some days, we ache for things which are out of reach.
Some days, we feel as though we could conquer the world.
Some days, we feel as though we don't even matter in this
big world.

And on all those days, we are just as worthy of love as we
are on our best days.

Summer

When was the last time you truly enjoyed summer?
Will you allow yet another summer to pass without enjoy-
ing it to the fullest?
Working late, heading home to bed, exhausted, worn down,
in pain.
Rarely taking walks, or pausing for a sunset.
Surely no fun trips.
Very few hikes.
Little time in the sun.
Nope, not this year.
This summer, I am healing.
And part of healing looks like enjoying this season.
No longer working such crazy hours in such a heavy job,
I actually have time to enjoy summer.
Routine walks and watching the sun set and the fireflies
appear.
Planting flowers and watching them begin to grow,
Even as I grow, too.
Floating down the river on the weekend, relaxing.
(Wait, have I finally allowed that word a space in my voca-
bulary and my life?)
Relaxing.
It's not lazy to care for yourself.
And sometimes caring for yourself means a day by the
pool, soaking up that vitamin D.
Sometimes it means a long hike through the woods,

beside a babbling brook, allowing the peace of nature to
wash over you.
Sometimes it means a day trip with a friend.
Or a couple hours at the dog park,
Watching my sweet girl run and play with her friends.
I don't remember the last time
I enjoyed summer this much—
The warmth, the joy, the peace, the refreshment.
Healing is a journey, and enjoying this summer is just a
piece of my journey.

Victoria Grace Gehman

Masterpiece in the Mess

Strokes of the paint brush–
Painting over me for the hundredth time.
Not even sure who I am anymore, beneath all these layers.
What if we could somehow erase the paint, peel back the
layers?
What would we find?
Would we be ruined,
Or might there still be beauty?
Even if it's a different kind of beauty–
Unique and messy.
Subtle and bold.
No need to hide–
Don't even try to paint over me one more time, I say
As I take back the brush and paint new strokes–
Not caring how others perceive them.
I am unique and my authenticity is a gift.
Not everyone can see the intricate designs
between the paint smears.
But I will wait for those who can.
Get your own canvas.
Find your own beauty.
Believe that you're a masterpiece.

Rest

They told me to rest and do the things that I enjoy.
But what is rest? How do I do it?
What do I enjoy? Do I even have hobbies anymore?
I found myself needing to answer these questions.
I had been working myself nearly to death for so long.
Any hobbies I once had were nearly forgotten.
I seemed incapable of stillness.
Until my body and my mental health left me with no choice
but to slow down.
Considerably. In a dramatic way.
What makes me smile?
I've slowly begun to rediscover my passions and hobbies.
My life now looks so different from my life a few months
ago.
So different, in fact, that it's barely recognizable.
Slowly–
and with many deep breaths and missteps along the way–
I am learning to listen to my body.
I am learning that I, too, am worth the rest and care it
takes to heal.

Victoria Grace Gehman

A Prayer for Hurting Friends

When it doesn't seem as though there is an end in sight,
When you aren't sure if you have it in you still to fight,
May you feel His comfort, wrapping you tightly,
Holding your pain nightly.
May you find yourself enveloped in the love of friends
who stay—
Even when your pain doesn't seem to go away.

Outgrowing Spaces

There are spaces and places
Where I used to fit,
People I used to enjoy being with.
But now, I no longer thrive in those same spaces and pla-
ces,
Or with those same peoples.
And for this, I grieve,
While, simultaneously, delighting in my growth–
For these both–
They can be true at the same time.
Grief and growth.
Sadness and delight.
For I miss the life I once had,
But not enough to go back.
For these new spaces, places, and peoples aren't so bad.
In fact, they are healthier.
And I am happier.

Finding Hope in New Seasons

Victoria Grace Gehman

Reaching for the Light

Some mornings we wake up,

And all we see is darkness.

Darkness may be all we feel in our hearts, too.

But then the sun rises,

And we reach, slowly,

For the light.

We reach for the light pouring through our windows,

We reach to feel the warmth of the sun on our skin.

And we reach, deep into the depths of our souls

To find some light there too.

Some days, we don't have to reach very far.

But other days, the light seems so far off.

Arms outstretched, we don't think we can reach that ray of

sunshine,

But then we start to feel its warmth

Even though it is so high up in the sky.

And its warmth brings light to our weary souls.

We reach for the light–

The joy, the hope, the gratitude–

Even on the days where the light seems to be gone,

We know it's just behind the clouds somewhere.

And it will return again.

So we keep on reaching

Reaching for the light.

So we keep on reaching
Reaching for the light.

Victoria Grace Gehman

Fully Alive

As the colors and sounds of spring return,
It feels as though the earth is coming alive again–
Fully alive.
As the barrenness of winter slowly begins to disappear
And bright flowers, green leaves, and the sounds of birds
chirping take its place,
We are reminded once again:
Winter does not last forever,
Joy still returns.
The fresh breeze, the sunshine,
the little critters reappearing–
All of this reminds us that the harshness of winter,
Is only for a season.
And yes, this season repeats itself on a regular basis–
Sometimes our seasons of suffering repeat themselves quite
often, too.
Sometimes these seasons last longer than usual–
Sometimes winter does that too.
As the hope of spring brings hope and warmth to my soul,
I smile a little more, offer random acts of kindness, and
walk with a lighter step.
I begin to live fully alive,
Cherishing each day of this season–
Where I have the capacity to live more fully alive

And to bring glimpses of life and hope to those neglected–
Whether that be plants or people.
So tend those gardens; plant new flowers.
Tend to your own soul; plant seeds of hope.
Live fully alive.

Victoria Grace Gehman

What If

What if...? We ask this question so much.
What if... I fail?
What if... I never heal?
What if... they leave?
What if... these dreams never happen?
What if... we get sick?
What if... we get hurt?
What if... someone we care about gets sick or hurt?
What if...And the list goes on.
And on. And on.
But what if... things could go right?
What if... it could be beautiful?
What if... you could find glimpses of joy and hope?
What if... they might actually understand? And stay?
What if... life wouldn't always hurt this bad?
What if... that next thing you're looking forward to
You could just simply cherish,
Instead of worrying about all the negative what ifs?
What if... we changed our negative what ifs
to positive what ifs?
What if... we looked for the beauty?
What if... we imagined the joyful moments to come?
What if... when we looked at the future we saw hope and
dreamed big?

What if... those big dreams could come true?
What if... we could actually heal?
And what if... it would actually be worth it?
Just take a moment and imagine the hopeful,
joyous what ifs.

How Much I've Grown

When I think about how much I've grown
And all the grace I've been shown,
My heart just bursts with gratitude
Passions and dreams have come alive –
I have found courage to believe and to achieve,
To be vulnerable and to make a difference,
However small, in the lives of other weary souls, so like my
own.
Even after all the storms,
I am still standing.
And I am stronger, braver, freer,
Than I ever imagined possible.
I am becoming who I was always meant to be,
And I no longer hate the person that I am.
To think that I could ever reach this place –
It's completely grace.

Slices of Heaven on Earth

Rays of sunshine, meandering creeks, dripping ice cream
cones–
A slice of heaven on earth.
The sound of laughter mixed with the aroma
of fresh coffee –
A slice of heaven o earth.
A friend who stays through your worst days, wrapping her
arms around you–
A slice of heaven on earth.
A church where all are welcomed and a chorus of voices
from various languages and backgrounds all sing toge-
ther–
A slice of heaven on earth.
Let each tiny slice of heaven on earth
point you to the future–
A real heaven where life is perfect, all are welcome, and
tears and pain are no more.

Victoria Grace Gehman

<u>Support</u>

Be my strong when I am weak.
Be my steady when I start to waver.
Be my gentle breeze when the heat blazes too hot.
Be my rock to grip when I'm falling.
Be my tight hug when I'm lonely.
Be my laughter when I'm sad.
Be my arms when I can't get back up.
Be my warmth when the elements leave me shivering.
Be my hope when I thought all hope was lost.
Be my shelter in the storm.
Be my shoulder to cry on when no one else even notices
I'm down.
Be my authentic when others are fake.
Be my journal when I cannot find the words.
Be my warmth when the fire dies down.
Be my other half when I don't feel whole.

& I'll be that for you, too.

<u>If You're Still Here</u>

And if you're still here,
Maybe it's because you've not yet seen
all you were meant to see,
You've not yet healed as much as you'll eventually
be able to heal,
You've not yet loved and been loved
as fully and deeply as you someday will,
You've not yet met every soul you're destined to meet,
You've not yet experienced every adventure
and small joy in store for you,
You've not yet fulfilled the entirety
of your purpose in this life,
You've not yet discovered all the happy you'll someday find
even in the midst of the struggle,
You've not yet traveled all the roads
meant for you to travel,
You've not yet gone before those who are to come after
you.
So stay.
Stay here.
Here is where you are meant to be.

Victoria Grace Gehman

Under the Stars

Under the stars
The sky seems to stretch for an eternity,
Possibilities are endless.
Something about those twinkling lights, the cool breeze–
It makes me believe.

It looks like millions, billions of stars–
More than I can count.
If even all these stars matter,
I must matter too.
I am one tiny star out of billions,
But I may be the one that someone sees on their darkest
nights.

<u>Fresh Winter Air</u>

The fresh winter air, so chill,
The woods, silent and still,
The snowfall, quiet and peaceful,
The woods, oh so beautiful.
There's something about a frigid early morning hike,
Before the world has yet awakened.
It's difficult to explain, but somehow the crisp air and the
slow steps through soft snow give clarity to the mind,
Stop racing thoughts,
And force me, along with all of nature,
To be still, to breathe deeply, inhaling the comfort
of the winter air,
Surrendering to peace and rest.

Victoria Grace Gehman

I Write These Words

I write these words–
Words of encouragement, words of hope–
I write these words.
And yet I'm not sure if I even believe these words
I'm writing.
I write them for you.
But I also write them for me –
So that maybe someday I'll slowly come
to believe these words.
I write these words–
Authentic, vulnerable words.
I write these words,
Even though they are often difficult for me to share.
Because I want you to know that you are not alone.
And that it is okay.
And I want to know that I am not alone, too.
And that it will be okay for me, also.
So I will keep writing–
Writing these words,
Until I can believe these words.
And then I will write some more.
Because there will always be someone else
who needs these words.
Even if it's just one person–
That is enough for me to know that my words matter.

<u>Treasure the Good Days</u>

And so, I treasure the good days
The ones that feel like sunshine rays.
Because you never know what the next day will bring.
One day life might feel fun,
And the next, you just want to be done.
Each day is such a fleeting thing.
Changing ever so quickly,
It's oh so slippery.
And so, to the happy moments I cling.
Because without those memories to hold onto,
I don't know what I would do
On those days where all I feel is the sting –
The sting from a life that is often hard and cold.
But I dare to be bold.
And as I treasure the good days, my heart begins to sing.

Hope

A burst of hope– or at least I assume it's hope.
I'm not sure I can recall what hope feels like.
Sudden and surprising– for I am not accustomed
to this feeling.
But it's rejuvenating–
Could I possibly begin to believe that there is hope for me?
That someday my life won't be filled with long drives to
new doctors, new medications, new questions, new diagno-
ses, new procedures, new pain...
That someday I might walk into this building and say,
"I feel so much better,"
Rather than sitting in the car willing the stabbing pains to
cease so I can enter the building–
With its cold walls and harsh, medical feel,
Hoping that here I will be well-cared for and validated.
Thankful for the few who have shown kindness
in their care for me.
But also hesitant, because of all those who have not.
So tentatively, I begin to hope for answers and
healing to this pain,
Yet I also hesitate to believe because this pain has been my
life for so many years.

<u>Peace</u>

This feeling of total contentment,
The feeling of not having looked at the clock in hours,
Not needing to rush or follow a schedule,
Just taking life moment by moment,
This feeling of joy,
And wonder at the tiniest details of nature,
This feeling of gratitude, not taking any of this
for granted–
What are these feelings? I wonder.
And I think to myself,
This just might be what it feels like to be at peace.
My body doesn't ache so much, my mind is quieted,
my soul is happy.
Peace?
Yep, I think it's peace.
And I wish I could share a piece of it with you,
So you might understand why I never want to leave these
mountains and this company.

Twenty-Four

I truly did not think that I would make it this far,
But here I am.
Twenty-four.
Another year has passed,
Even harder than the last.
Pain and hurt often seemed to prevail,
It felt like it was always one thing after another.
You know that feeling, right?
When nothing ever seems to go right?
And when it does, you worry it won't last
Or that a tragedy will be next.
So much heaviness.
And yet.
I've learned to appreciate the smallest glimpses of joy.
I've allowed others to hold on to hope for me
when I couldn't.
I'm learning to slow down.
I'm beginning to believe that I am worth caring for.
So many beautiful moments would have been missed.
If I hadn't stayed alive.
I'm moving to a new, more spacious apartment.
I published a book.
I adopted a puppy.
I was gifted with some authentic friendships.
I've made progress in healing.
Even in the storms,
Even in the hurricanes,

Even in the days of darkness that turned into seasons,
The story is not over.
And now I'm moving on to the next chapter,
Grateful.
And filled with more hope than I've had in a very long
time.

Victoria Grace Gehman

Echo

Echo. Echo.
Once, I said to myself, "You failed."
And now it's an echo inside of my head–
Like a record that's stuck, or a song on repeat–
Infinitely.
You failed, you failed.
Echo. Echo.
But then you meet me right here–
In this echoing cave,
Beneath the stalactites, beside the stalagmites.
And you say to me:
You are loved and lovable.
And those five words–
They echo, too.
Quietly, at first. Then gradually increasing in volume.
You are loved. You are lovable.
Echo. Echo.
May the voice echoing in your head today be a voice of love.

Seesaws

Finally feeling like I am no longer caught between one
extreme or the other–
Like things are slowly balancing out.
The seesaw was always either way up or way down.
Either I was flying off of it in excitement
or slamming to the ground.
Never just in the middle.
But now, I am beginning to notice peace and a settling–
A balancing of this seesaw of life.

Victoria Grace Gehman

Honesty

When our honesty is met with disbelief and rejection, it
becomes easier to simply silence our voices.
Speaking up about injustices or trauma
takes immense courage,
And when the response is less than favorable,
it only adds to the damage we feel.
So we stay silent.
We lose our voices.
But the silence kills us slowly– starting from the inside.
No one can see our pain, but inside there's a raging beast–
One that wants to scream and shout the truth
from the tops of the hills.
But we can't.
So it starts to eat us up.
Our mental health suffers. We may begin experiencing
physical symptoms.
We feel alone. We become isolated.
We long for someone to hear our truths, to believe our
story.
But we are too afraid that we will be met with disbelief
and rejection, yet again.
Sometimes it feels like too big a risk to take–
Until staying silent becomes even more of a risk.
Honesty is freeing.
To tell our story and be believed lifts heavy boulders
from our shoulders.
To tell our story can help others find the courage
to tell theirs, too.

<u>Hope in Changing Seasons</u>

To hope we will cling,
When we don't know what the next day will bring,
When our weary souls glimpse those first signs of spring,
When our hearts rejoice and can't help but sing,
When the sun sinks down,
When frost covers the ground,
Will we believe that all the lost will still be found,
That the world will still keep spinning 'round?
When clouds pour down seemingly endless rain,
When all we feel is pain,
When we're fighting to stay sane,
In all these changing seasons, hope– it remains.

Thank you for Reading!

As a self-published author, it's a little bit like owning a small business. By purchasing this book, you are directly supporting me– and my pup. Each purchase means so much to me, and each share also makes a tremendous difference. Please share my book with friends and leave a review on Amazon or Goodreads. Reviews make more of a difference than you may realize and help me to increase awareness of not only this book but also my name as an author. If this book encouraged you, I would love to hear from you. You can connect with me on Instagram @writetoreconnect. Follow me on Instagram for more poetry, updates on future books, and glimpses into my own life – including hiking and nature photography.

If you enjoyed this book...

You may also enjoy my first poetry collection entitled "Slow Your Pace, Hope a Little Longer," which is available on Amazon.

www.ingramcontent.com/pod-product-compliance
Lightning Source LLC
Chambersburg PA
CBHW060254150626
46553CB00019BA/2276